Crayola
FALL COLORS

Mari Schuh

Lerner Publications ◆ Minneapolis

IN MEMORY OF EVELYN QUAM

Official Licensed Product
Lerner Publications Company
A division of Lerner Publishing Group, Inc.
241 First Avenue North
Minneapolis, MN 55401 USA

For reading levels and more information, look up this title at www.lernerbooks.com.

Main body text set in Billy Infant Regular 24/36.
Typeface provided by SparkyType.

Library of Congress Cataloging-in-Publication Data

Names: Schuh, Mari C., 1975-
Title: Crayola fall colors / by Mari Schuh.
Description: Minneapolis : Lerner Publications, [2018] | Series: Crayola seasons | Audience: Age 4-9. | Audience: K to grade 3. | Includes bibliographical references and index.
Identifiers: LCCN 2016044742 (print) | LCCN 2016045539 (ebook) | ISBN 9781512432916 (lb : alk. paper) | ISBN 9781512455731 (pb : alk. paper) | ISBN 9781512449297 (eb pdf)
Subjects: LCSH: Autumn—Juvenile literature. | Seasons—Juvenile literature. | Crayons—Juvenile literature.
Classification: LCC QB637.7 .S378 2018 (print) | LCC QB637.7 (ebook) | DDC 535.6—dc23

LC record available at https://lccn.loc.gov/2016044742

Manufactured in the United States of America
1-41822-23782-12/15/2016

TABLE OF CONTENTS

LEAVES IN FALL

The air is cool.

The wind blows colorful leaves all around.

Fall is here!

What colors

4

do you see?

In fall, green leaves change color.

They turn bright yellow, orange, and red.

They turn deep purple and brown too.

Dry, crunchy leaves float to the ground.

You can draw leaves. Try adding texture with small dots.

What happens when you draw
many dots close together?

Soon most trees are bare.

Bright feathers stand out on the branches.

Some colors are bright.

They stand out from dull colors.

Which of these colors
stand out to you?

PREPARING FOR WINTER

In fall, animals get ready for the snowy winter.

Chipmunks gather red berries and brown nuts.

Knitted hats and scarves keep you warm in the fall.

Knitted yarn has a pattern of straight and curved lines.

What kind of lines can you draw?

FALL ON THE FARM

Farmers harvest crops. Machines gather yellow corn and golden wheat from the fields.

Red apples are ripe and ready to be picked.

The bright sun makes shadows in the orchard.

You can add shadows to a drawing.

First, press down lightly with a crayon or colored pencil. Then press harder.

FALL FUN

In fall, people celebrate Halloween with glowing orange jack-o'-lanterns.

What colors do you use to celebrate fall?

WORLD OF COLORS

The world is filled with so many colors. Here are some Crayola® crayon colors used in this book. Can you find them in the photos? What colors do you see in fall?

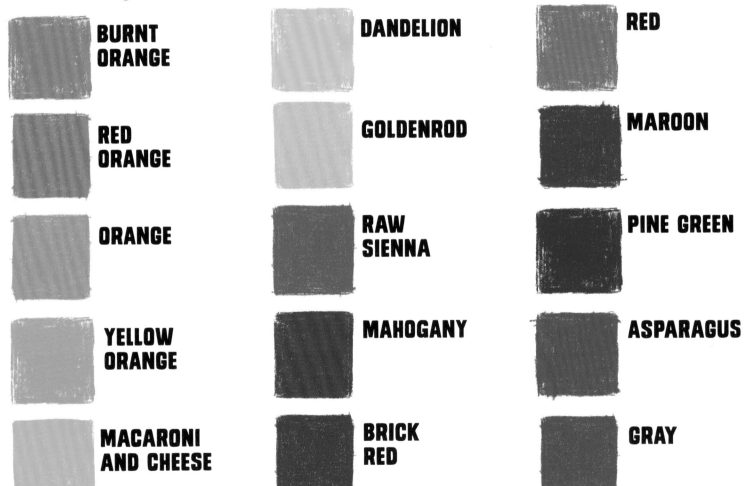

BURNT ORANGE

RED ORANGE

ORANGE

YELLOW ORANGE

MACARONI AND CHEESE

DANDELION

GOLDENROD

RAW SIENNA

MAHOGANY

BRICK RED

RED

MAROON

PINE GREEN

ASPARAGUS

GRAY

GLOSSARY

dull: not bright or colorful

harvest: to gather crops that are ripe

jack-o'-lantern: a pumpkin with a painted or carved face. Candles are often put inside jack-o'-lanterns.

knitted: made by looping yarn together with special needles or by machine

orchard: a field or farm where fruit trees are grown

pattern: a repeated form or design

ripe: fully grown

texture: the look and feel of an object

TO LEARN MORE

BOOKS

Dils, Tracey E. *Falling Leaves 1, 2, 3: An Autumn Counting Book*. Mankato, MN: Amicus Readers, 2016. Explore this colorful season by counting different fall objects.

Plourde, Lynn. *Bella's Fall Coat*. New York: Disney-Hyperion, 2016. Read this fun story about Bella, a girl who loves the colors and sounds of fall.

Schuh, Mari. *I See Fall Leaves*. Minneapolis: Lerner Publications, 2017. Learn about the colors, shapes, and parts of fall leaves.

WEBSITES

Let in the Leaves
http://www.crayola.com/crafts/let-in-the-leaves-craft
Create a colorful work of art using leaf rubbings and leaf prints in this fun activity.

Why Leaves Change Color Video
http://www.maine.gov/dacf/mfs/projects/fall_foliage/kids/movie.html
Learn how fall leaves change color.

INDEX

PHOTO ACKNOWLEDGMENTS

The images in this book are used with the permission of: © iStockphoto.com/gordana jovanovic, p. 1 (background leaves wood); © Todd Strand/Independent Picture Service, (crayons throughout); © iStockphoto.com/miteemaus5, p. 2; © iStockphoto.com/Ron Thomas, pp. 4–5; © iStockphoto.com/PeteMuller, p. 6; © iStockphoto.com/tbralnina, p. 7; © Royalty-Free/CORBIS, p. 8; © iStockphoto.com/layritten, p. 9 (stipple pattern tiles); © iStockphoto.com/pchoui, p. 10; © npine/Shutterstock.com, pp. 12–13; © iStockphoto.com/Richard Bowden, p. 14; © Casadphoto/Dreamstime.com, pp. 16–17; © iStockphoto.com/Jorge Salcedo, p. 18; © iStockphoto.com/Virtaa, p. 19 (apple outline); © ChuckPlace/iStock/Thinkstock, pp. 20–21.

Cover: © iStockphoto.com/Sun_Time.

LERNER
SOURCE

Expand learning beyond the printed book. Download free, complementary educational resources for this book from our website, www.lerneresource.com.